A Quest For Absolute Power

~ Inspiration is finding God's Truth ~

With
The Final Quest

James Charles Bouffard, Psy.D., Ph.D.

(Edited by: Lisa Diane Branscome)

Second Edition

Illustrated

Lynn Paulo Foundation
Pomona, California

ISBN 978-0-6152-0163-4

Printed in the United States of America

Other works by Dr. Bouffard:

Be A Private Investigator
The Magician's Fight!
The Entrepreneurial Ben Franklin
Defiance! A Saga of David Crockett and the Alamo

Dedicated to:
Robert "Bob" Phillips
An inspiration for this work.

Contents

Miscellaneous

Illustrations List

Following page 38:

- Pope John XIX [May, 1024 – October, 1032].
- Pope Benedict IX [1032 – 1044, 1045, 1047 – 1048].
- Pope Leo X [March 11, 1513 – December 2, 1521].
- Spanish Inquisition.
- Pope Adrian VI [January 9, 1522 – September 14, 1523]
- Martin Luther (1483 – 1546).
- Church of Santa Maria dell'Anima, Rome.
- Pope John XXIII [October 28, 1958 – June 3, 1963].
- Pope Paul VI [June 21, 1963 – August 6, 1978].
- Pope John Paul I [August 26, 1978 – September 29, 1978].
- Pope John Paul II with future Pope Benedict XVI.
- Benjamin Franklin (1706 – 1790).

"Some people want to see God with their eyes as they see a cow, and to love Him as they love their cow — for the milk and cheese, and the profit it brings them. This is how it is with people who love God for the sake of outward wealth and inward comfort. They do not rightly love God, when they love Him for their own advantage. Indeed, I tell you the truth, any object you have in your mind, however good, will be a barrier between you and the utmost truth."

Eckhart von Hochheim
Meister Eckhart
(ca 1260 – ca 1327)
German Theologian

In 1327, Meister Eckhart was accused of heresy by the Franciscan-led Inquisition and subsequently tried by order of decadent Avignon Pope John XXII.

Though Eckhart purportedly died prior to a verdict, no record marking the means or exact date of his death has ever been discovered.

A Quest For Absolute Power

Prologue

From his very beginning man has struggled for truth through some form of religion.

Unfortunately, one accepted creed traveled through time unacceptable to any basic truth.

For nearly two thousand years mankind's search for truth lay hindered by a religion, which was not a religion in any sense of truism, but merely personal entertainment without much meaning. Such a religion, or ritual, employed thoughts by man to appease himself. Not God, nor **God's Truth**!

The Roman Catholic Church had long ago accepted man's thoughts over God's, creating their own form of worship. This was often a deceptive, if not clearly a dishonest route to theocentric ethics — needed in a successful search for **God's Truth**.

Unhappily, this conventional religion had, through years of ecclesiastical abuse lost her "religious mind," leaving believers to grope alone in darkness for any sign of light.

Etymologically, "religious mind" signified "A state of being bound to that which is **Noble**, to that which is **Great**... That one had to live a diligent, scrupulous and honest existence... **That God is the Truth, the Light, the Way**." Yet all that changed, although gradually at first, as this religion replaced God's laws with man's.

Cleric's and prelates waved God aside as they interpreted His meaning of life to benefit themselves in their quest for worldly riches — for **absolute power**.

The result? Integrity and ethics were lost through following misdirected tenets created by man, if falsely attributed to God. These dogmas have been instrumental in clouding **God's Truth**, in clouding our human compassion, in putting an end to organized "religious mind."

Clarification

Although the preceding and following writings may appear a denigration of the Roman Catholic Church, this author would like it readily understood no such intention is allocated with baseness. Her actions are subject to recorded history, leaving her open to thorough examination. Please keep this in mind as you read *A Quest For Absolute Power* and *The Final Quest*.

In studying for the Roman Catholic priesthood during his youth, this author took it upon himself to delve deeper into Church background than wished by his tutor. As a result, he moved away. Not from the Church per se, but from Church authority in her claim of an all-encompassing path to faith.

"Hence from all we have hitherto said, it is clear, beloved Catholics, that we cannot approve the opinions which some [Protestants, Jews and other heretics] comprise under the head of Americanism [freedom]."

Pope Leo XIII

(1810 – 1903)

[Pope: 1878 – 1903]

Chapter 1

The thousand years which followed Christ's crucifixion brought Christianity to its horrific zenith. By 1033 C.E., we had forgotten almost entirely why we were called Christians. Pope Benedict IX was waging war against heretics, loving his mistresses, and writing his own laws as **Supreme Head of the Christian World**. While his priestly minions paraded the countryside singing praises for His Holiness.

In 1032, his father Count Alberic III elevated Count Theophylactus of Tusculum, historically recognized as boy-Pope Benedict IX, to papal dignity.

The 20-year-old ascended Peter's chair vacated by the death of his uncle, Pope John XIX, taking command of the Roman Catholic Church which then stood sovereign to the Christian world.

From that year until his forced abdication in 1048 plunder, murder, oppression, and immoral lust directed his reign. A direction that would lead to the break up of the Roman Catholic Church and split all organized religions into a diffused, meaningless jumble, still searching ineffectually for a theocratic truth.

A search continuing through one hundred and twelve future pontiffs and numerous sectarian religious leaders, slowing to a measure with Pope John XXIII (1958 – 1965) who attempted to bring Catholics, non-Catholics, and Jews together as one family, proclaiming it was "every person's right to worship God in accordance with the dictates of his or her own conscience and to profess his or her religion both in private and public." He further decreed human beings to "have rights from God that no one can take from them."

This was in early spring of 1963. Already suffering Roman Curia [1] criticism for winning the Soviet's **Balzan Peace Prize** in March, in which they labeled him a crypto-communist, his big, loving heart nearly broke when the council clashed over his *Pacem in Terris*, calling for a unity of all religions under one God.

Bending under the weight of this unjust adjudication of his faith, he took to his bed with a stomach ailment on May 23, 1963. His doctors, Valdoni and Mazzoni, diagnosed internal hemorrhaging caused by a lesion in his stomach lining. Then peritonitis set in, and he was given the last rites.

On May 28th, he sustained a heart attack and was allowed only hours to live. It was also learned the pope had endured an inoperable stomach cancer for the past year without public complaint.

Special prayers filled the air in every continent.

Surprisingly, he rallied.

Sitting up and drinking black coffee, he joked with his doctors and secretary.

The world was beginning to wonder.

But, on May 31st, the Vatican broke the news. For Pope John XXIII, death within a short time was imminent.

On Saturday and Sunday, he slipped in and out of a coma. Each time he regained consciousness, he managed a cherubic smile. At one point quipping to Dr. Mazzoni: "Don't worry. My bags are packed and I am ready."

On Monday evening, June 3, 1963, around 7:30 p.m. he murmured a favorite prayer, which ended with "...that they may all be one." At 7:49 p.m. he closed his eyes and went to God.

Teleprinters, telephones, and televisions spread the sad news around the waiting world.

Catholics, Protestants, Orthodox, Jews, Buddhists, Moslems, believers and atheists wept in unison for the man who had made goodness and holiness attractive to everyone.

Before Angelo Roncalli emerged as Pope John XXIII, the Roman Catholic Church condemned diverse religions with a vengeance. Jews, especially, were denounced for their actions against God — in the personage of Jesus Christ.

Pope John XXIII was the first pope ever verbally attacked by his own church agencies when he allowed for "audiences without prejudice." The Church, however, back-pedaled when they discovered this pope, unlike his predecessors, cared little for what anyone thought but God. And God, he believed, is a forgiving God. As mankind should be a universally forgiving race.

Unfortunately, John's pontificate lasted just short of five years. Not enough time to reverse wholly over a thousand years of ecclesiastical damage.

Who would succeed John? And would he continue to apply humanism to the Roman Church? Or would he revert and stay with traditional canon law, decrying whatever altruistic edicts his predecessor bequeathed.

Both Vatican City and the world held its breath.

Chapter 2

On June 21, 1963, white smoke plumed from a stove-pipe chimney atop the Sistine Chapel.

As the watching throng in St. Peter's Square roared **Viva IL Papa**, Alfredo Cardinal Ottaviani, senior Cardinal Deacon, stepped onto the balcony with a little group of cardinals and officials and raised his hand for silence.

"Giovanni Battista Cardinal Montini of Milan takes the name of Paul VI," he announced.

An hour later a 63-year-old man of medium height, slight build, and milky blue eyes appeared on the loggia and blessed the crowd.

To the Curia's dismay, he repeated words spoken several days before the papal conclave opened for election:

"Pope John XXIII pointed out some landmarks which it will be wise not only to remember but to follow. How could we deviate from the path he blazed?"

Consonant cheers erupted in the square below.

The Church's renewal and inner purification was to persist under the new pope.

Fifteen years later Pope John Paul I stepped out to the loggia, promised to continue the works of John XXIII and Paul VI, then returned to the shadows of the Vatican. He was never to reemerge. Dying, it was rumored, by an altered bottle of a low-blood-pressure medication called Effortil.

Dismissing these rumors the conclave, in a surprising motion, elected Karol Wojtyla the first non-Italian Pontiff in 456 years.

In their attempt to return to absolute power they had decided a foreigner best for the job. Cardinal Wojtyla could be controlled as they had Dutch Pope Adrian VI in 1522.

When Netherlands-born Adrian Dedel, living in Spain, learned of his election as pope he was frightened. His predecessor, Leo X, had died mysteriously in December following a bare altercation with the Church over the rebellious Martin Luther. He was only forty-six, and well liked by the Curia. What would happen to a pope only known to a few Spanish cardinals, and not at all in Rome?

What did they want him for? Was he brought in to lead the fight against a fellow Germanic, whose little group was referred to as "Lutherans" in Pope Leo X's last Bull? What would happen if he failed to stop the Protestant Reformation, still threatening to split the Church?

Would the Curial bureaucracy seek to control his steps? Would he function solely as a puppet, strung to advisers who presented him with wishes and recommendations?

Would he be murdered if he rejected their council?

These fears kept him away from Rome for six months ensuing the election. He felt safe in Spain. In Spain, he was the power. As Grand Inquisitor since November of 1516, he had presided over more than 20, 000 heretical trials. In Rome, he would be a figurehead. An expendable figurehead.

Meanwhile, Martin Luther, the excommunicated Catholic friar, raised his voice in Germany against the new pope making his way slowly to Rome. Reviling Adrian as the Anti-Christ "through whom Satan speaks."

Adrian countered by calling Luther "…a second Mahomet who allowed priests to marry. His conduct is a godless zeal against the priesthood. His followers are infamous folks."

Urged by the Curia, Adrian continued to attack Luther in an attempt to heal Germany's split from the Church.

Without much success.

Not only was Germany rearing back, Spain and even Italy threatened opposition.

The Church was deteriorating from the inside. The Roman Curia knew this, yet kept silent. If Adrian were unable to stop the Reform, they would find someone who could.

"Men never do evil so completely and cheerfully as when they do it from religious conviction."
Blaise Pascal
French mathematician and theologian
(1623 – 1662)

Chapter 3

In autumn of 1522, the Great Plague of Rome carried off 100 victims daily. Adrian, tortured with self-reproach over the Reformation issue — feeling God had sent this affliction to punish him for not standing up to the Curia — turned to one of his Flemish advisers, who simply said:

"The Church has no more destructive enemies than the popes. For their execrable lives, they murder Christ again."

Adrian stood and paced the marbled floor. Basically a good and pious man, he blamed himself for the deaths of innocent Romans stricken as only an angered god could strike. He had originally been persuaded to accept the position as Grand Inquisitor through a weakness of the flesh. A later penchant for power overshadowing a youthful proclivity to follow the genteel teachings of Christ.

For several months Adrian remained stagnant in the Papal States, unable to act or even discuss measures against the plague, the Reformation — nor the Turkish concern — with local authorities. No one in Rome trusted the ponderous, dull-witted Germanic pontiff they dubbed "The Barbarian."

His cardinals, prelates and functionaries of the Curia had fled to safety in the hills of northern Italy, deserting the very people needing their comfort.

Finally, Adrian made his decision, the Roman Curia, not the Reformation, should be stopped. For Christendom to survive, the Church needed to purge herself even at the risk of a universal break-up.

During the winter, he prepared to take action.

Conferring with his papal legate, Francesco Chieregati, he handed him a written **Self-Accusation of the Papacy** for delivery to the Nuremberg Diet. He hoped to quell the overheated ambience sweeping the Germanic states.

"We frankly acknowledge," went the confession, "that God has allowed this persecution to come upon the Church [1] because of the sins of mankind, especially those of the priests and prelates... Scripture testifies loudly and forcefully that the sins of the people manifest in the sins of the priests, and therefore our Redeemer, as Chrysostom [2] says, when He wanted to heal the sick city of Jerusalem, went first to the temple to punish the sins of the priests, just as a good physician heals first the root of the disease. We know that some years ago much that were abominable happened at this Holy See. Abuses occurred, authorities exceeded their powers, until all turned toward evil deeds. And it is not surprising that the disease should have spread from the head to the members; from the popes to the prelates. All of us, prelates and clergy, have strayed from the path of right, and there is not one who does good...

"Therefore, each one of us must see whence he has fallen, and must rather judge himself than expose himself to judgment by God with the rod of His wrath...

"Therefore we must promise in our name that we will make every effort to see that first of all the Court of Rome [3], from which possibly all these evils have taken rise, is reformed. Then, as the disease began here, so will the cure. To this undertaking we feel ourselves the more bound in that the whole world craves such a reform...

"Yet no one should be surprised if we do not end all these abuses with one single blow. For the sickness is deep-rooted and takes many forms. We must therefore advance step by step...

"We will show Christendom the way. We are aware of the torture of the cross, which meets the Lord again and again, and us too who let it loose, we ourselves being both torturers and victims. We know also the cleansing, the amendments, and the bliss of faith...

"Have confidence with us that together we shall overcome the powers of darkness..."

With this parchment of admission, Pope Adrian VI signed his death warrant.

"If the pope is going to get rid of the abuses step by step, perhaps a whole century will elapse between one step and the next," thundered the irascible Luther from Germany.

In Rome, the Curia raged over their loss of control and plotted against Adrian.

In March of 1523 an attempt was made on his life. An attempt which failed when the Curia member suddenly turned the dagger on himself.

Adrian further enraged the Curia when he addressed the Consistory in May:

"… If by the Roman Church you mean its head or pontiff, it is beyond question that he can err even in matters touching the faith. He does this when he teaches heresy by his own judgment or decretal. In truth, many Roman pontiffs were heretics…"

The following two months saw unrest in Rome tantamount to civil war. Christians against Christians. Bishops and cardinals against the pope.

Throughout Europe, Reformers, kings, princes, subjects, citizens and peasants clashed, moving south to the Eternal City.

On August 1st Adrian, fearing a Turkish invasion and an attack by northern Christians, initiated a defensive alliance with Holy Roman Emperor Charles V, Archduke Ferdinand of Austria, Cardinal de' Medici in Florence, the Duke of Milan and King Henry VIII of England, contrary to Curia counsel.

Two days later he felt sick, taking to his bed.

Immediately, plans to secure the election of Giulio Cardinal de' Medici [4] — who sided with any faction wielding power — were formed.

But the big Dutchman's constitution fooled everyone. He recovered on Sunday, August 4th, to celebrate Mass, sermonizing on the need for Church reform headed by the pope and the emperor.

On Tuesday, August 6th, he fell ill again. One month and eight days later he was dead. His body, like Leo X before him, lay swollen and covered with black patches.

His official papers vanished shortly after, and have yet to be discovered.

No tears were shed for Adrian VI. He was entombed quietly, then later transferred without ceremony to the German national church of Santa Maria dell' Anima, Rome.

Anonymously inscribed on the vault are the words:

Alas, even in the best of men, how much depends on the times in which he lives!

Had the *Curia Romana* studied their failure to restrain the Dutch pope, Adrian VI, they would not have been so quick in selecting Polish, Karol Cardinal Wojtyla, Pope John Paul II.

"Truth must be the foundation stone, the cement to so-
lidify the entire social edifice."

Pope John Paul II
(1920 – 2005)
[Pope: 1978 – 2005]

Chapter 4

When John Paul II ascended Peter's chair, he knew nothing of the danger he was placed in. Unlike Adrian VI, he had no fear of curial wiles. To him, he was elevated to pontification as God's design. Not as a nefarious scheme of man.

As a fact, Cardinal Wojtyla never expected to be pope. Even when he was chosen by Paul VI in 1976 to give a Lenten retreat and to hear the pope's confession did he consider the possibility? He was a Pole, and no Polish cardinal had ever risen to that exalted position.

His background seemed also against him. He was, as one Curia member argued, a non-conformist.

In opposition to Pope Pius XII's (1939 – 1958) advice, he had joined the resistance against Nazism. Later, he worked to save the lives of persecuted Jews in Krakow, Poland. Also disapproved by the Roman Church.

Could a man like that be controlled?

This, they found to their consternation, was hardly plausible.

Even the most liberal of prelates soon grew to dislike the rookie pontiff's intransigent attitude toward, in their eyes, canon authority. Instead of keeping with papal mystique, he was beginning to flaunt himself around the world. Like the actor he once was, he displayed himself center-stage and opened the Church to more criticism than had John XXIII, that crypto-communist who nearly swept her away with his foolish idea of theocentric ethics toward humanity.

This pope, too, would have to be stopped. The Roman Curia needed to rid itself of a mistake.

John Paul II, his eyes closed in prayer for every race and religion around the world, paid little notice to warnings that his Curia considered his actions bordering on heresy and planned assassination.

On May 13, 1981, that mission was all but accomplished for them when he was shot as his motorcade entered St. Peter's Square, requiring a 5 ½ hour operation, and six pints of blood, to save his life.

On May 12, 1982, one day to the anniversary of the May 13th attempt, a psychopathic ex-priest named Juan Fernández Y Krohn brandished a bayonet in the name of the Church-criticized **Second Vatican Council** [1], calling John Paul II an agent of Communist Moscow.

Two days after Christmas, 1983, the pope paid a visit to the prison where Mehmet Ali Ağca, a hired Turkish gunman, was serving a life sentence.

Speaking privately for twenty minutes with his would-be assassin of 1981, he emerged and told the waiting media "What we talked about will have to remain a secret between him and me. I spoke to him as a brother whom I have pardoned and who has my complete trust [2]."

Following his attempted assassinations, John Paul steeled himself against further assaults, but continued his presence as a globe-trotting voice for Christ, waving aside his growing ill health — and the Curia — as Church officials' love for comfort had long ago waved aside God.

Back home on April 13, 1986, he made an unexpected visit to the **Great Synagogue of Rome** on Lungotevere Cenci, joining Rabbi Elio Toaff in prayer.

His plan was to repair centuries of abusive Vatican-Jewish history, a work left unfinished by the death of Pope John XXIII, by underlining a determination to use his papacy to amend ties.

The Curia shook its collective head.

In January of 1995, as a diversion for Al-Qaeda-funded **Operation Bojinka** [3], John Paul was concerted for assassination once again.

A suicide bomber, disguised as a priest, was to amble up beside the popemobile as the motorcade passed en route to San Carlos Seminary in Makati City, Philippines — and detonate an explosion.

Both this and the main Bojinka plot, fortunately, were defeated when a chemical fire inadvertently ignited by the conspirators drew Filipino police attention on January 6th and 7th, leading to their arrests.

Unfortunately, the lessons learned from this disruptive error of 1995 were apparently applied to the September 11, 2001 attacks.

In 1998, the Curia remained silent as they watched the 78-year-old pontiff leave his sickbed for a triumphal tour of Cuba, and a heartfelt handshake with a man believed for years the Anti-Christ — Fidel Castro.

A young aid to President Castro, noticing the pope's slow, shuffling gait and trembling hands, would ask if he thought he should retire.

Unable to resist such a moment, the pope quipped with a humorous expression: "I don't run the Church with my feet or my hands, but with my mind!"

On March 12, 2000, John Paul delivered an unprecedented public statement not heard since 1522, imploring forgiveness for sins and faults committed or condoned by the Church in its two thousand years of existence.

The Curia, holding its breath, said and did nothing.

As the years moved on, John Paul walked unsteady as he used his crosier [4] for balance. His eyes were webbed, and the edges of his mouth twitched with pain.

His shoulders were rounded with the gravity of tenure beyond his age. And his skullcap covered the few hairs neatly combed each morning.

Still, beneath this all radiated an exuberance which pushed him to new extremes into this millennium.

Whether he perceived himself leading the Roman Church further into this century, we may never know. However, discernible evidence confirmed a man endeavoring to gather all faiths into a synergetic body by the end of the 20th century. To fulfill a legacy of truth in **God's Name**. To propel the Church from man's law of self-indulgence to **God's Law** of selfless sacrifice for the sake of humanity.

As he administered Mass at St. Peter's Basilica a circled dome, two hundred feet above his head, lettered words of the Lord: *"Tu es Petrus, et super hanc aedificado ecclesiam meam, et portae inferi non praevalebunt adversus eam"* ("Thou art Peter, and upon this rock I will build my church, and the gates of hell will not prevail against it.")

For Simon Peter the humanistic works established by Jesus would continue until his own martyred death in 64 C.E., but were not sustained by his successors.

Although considered the first pontiff by modern Catholic clergy and laity, early Church Fathers perceived Peter as a Jew, refusing to accept his teachings for the Christian world. Turning a blind eye to the fact that Jesus Christ, recognized founder of Christianity, lived and died a Jew.

Pope John Paul II held the "Text of Peter" in his hands as he prayed. To him, Peter's authority stemmed from the Lord.

Jesus Christ, Son of God in his mind, conferred upon Peter absolute power of the Church. Therefore, every papal successor should have adhered to His teachings. Teachings which would have brought theocentric ethics to a clouded ecclesiastical past.

Preparing his inherited office to cope with the twenty-first century, he remembered words spoken in 1962 by Maximos IV Saigh, patriarch of the Melkite Greek Catholic Church of Antioch. Words which paralleled John XXIII's thoughts, yet words forgotten until Pope John Paul II:

> *"...Let us open our eyes and be practical. Let us see things as they are and not as we would like them to be. Otherwise we risk speaking in a desert. What is at stake is the future of the Church's mission to the world..."*

Pope John Paul II brought a maturing Church nearly five years into the new millennium before the Lord received him home on April 2, 2005.

...May God protect and guide Pope Benedict XVI and all future pontiffs through the 21st century — and beyond.

"Let us love, not in word or speech, but in truth and action."
John 3:18

Romanus
(? – 1032 C.E.)
Pope John XIX
[May, 1024 – October, 1032]
(Image in author's collection)

Count Theophylactus of Tusculum
(1012 – ca 1065)
Pope Benedict IX
[1032 – 1044, 1045, 1047 – 1048]
(Image in author's collection)

Giovanni di Lorenzo de′ Medici
(1475 – 1521)
Pope Leo X
[March 11, 1513 – December 2, 1521]
(Image courtesy: Kean Collection)

Spanish Inquisition.
An accused heretic is broken on The Wheel, as priests look on in mock concern and prepare to record a possible confession. (Image in author's collection.)

POPE ADRIAN (HADRIAN) VI
(1522 - 1523)

Adrian Dedel
(1459 – 1523)
Pope Adrian VI
[January 9, 1522 – September 14, 1523]
(Image in author's collection)

Martin Luther
(1483 – 1546)
German Catholic friar, theologian, Protestant Reformer.
(Image courtesy: Thomas Fisher Rare Book Library)
(University of Toronto)

Church of Santa Maria dell' Anima, Rome.
Pope Adrian VI's remains were transferred to this final resting place on August 11, 1533. (Image in author's collection.)

Angelo Giuseppe Roncalli
(1881 – 1963)
Pope John XXIII
[October 28, 1958 – June 3, 1963]
(Image in author's collection)

Giovanni Battista Enrico Antonio Maria Montini
(1897 – 1978)
Pope Paul VI
[June 21, 1963 – August 6, 1978]
(Image in author's collection)

Albino Luciani
(1912 – 1978)
Pope John Paul I
[August 26, 1978 – September 29, 1978]
(Image in author's collection)

Pope John Paul II with future Pope Benedict XVI.
In 1981 Pope John Paul II called Joseph Cardinal Ratzinger to the Vatican. The two would have continued 90-minute weekly meetings, followed by leisurely luncheons. (Image in author's collection.)

Benjamin Franklin, ca 1780.
(1706 – 1790)
Businessman, inventor, scientist, statesman.
(Image courtesy: American Philosophical Society)

The
Final Quest

"Religion has not civilized man. Man has civilized religion."
Robert Green Ingersoll
American orator, freethinker, humanist
(1833 – 1899)

The Final Quest

Chapter 1

As the religious world accepted theocentric ethics in the late twentieth century, so too did our secular.

If, as we shall see, through a different path…

…A path fashioned in the cobblestone streets of 18th century Philadelphia, where 42-year-old Benjamin Franklin sits scribbling notes for ***Poor Richard's Almanac***, while his new business partner, David Hall, peers with amusement over his shoulder.

Suddenly, Franklin crumples one of the notes and throws it to the floor with a curse.

Bending to retrieve the fallen paper, Hall admonishes Ben his choice of words.

"For shame, Benjamin! What must your readers' consider

should they hear you speak such execrable language?"

"It's not the words that make the difference, David. It's the actions. The actions!"

Scratching his head in confusion, then shrugging in compliance to his strange friend, Hall returns to his own desk and remains silent.

Benjamin Franklin was well aware blasphemes meant little to a world leagues from church dogma.

As a boy in Boston, he sat for hours listening to the private preaching of Cotton Mather as the reverend remonstrated sins brought to mankind in its quest for mortal riches.

Growing to adulthood, he held two books uppermost in his mind.

One, a gift from the Reverend Mather, slammed commercial thoughts of man. The other, a merchant friend's book of accounts, brought into reality trade endeavors necessary for the survival of mankind.

As the years passed, he learned to combine the two registers of separate persuasions into a single concept followed by more businesses today in their search for the relief of earthly suffering than — sad to say — in his own time.

Nevertheless, Ben Franklin cleared the way for theocentric ethics in business. While profiting from his own efforts.

For your consideration, this author has submitted the following from his book, *The Entrepreneurial Ben Franklin*.

In these excerpts we'll see but a fraction of the contributions given us by a man who swore occasionally, yet let his actions prove him out:

The year was now 1732. George Washington was born in Bridges Creek, Virginia. George II was king of England. The first colony in Georgia was settling. Philadelphia was breaking ground for its State House, later known as Independence Hall. Deborah Franklin gave birth to a son, Francis Folger. And B. FRANKLIN was preparing to launch *Poor Richard's Almanac* [1].

By the age of 26, Ben's sights were fully aimed toward the public good. Of *Poor Richard's Almanac*, he wrote "I considered it a proper vehicle for conveying instruction among the common people, who bought scarcely any other books; I therefore filled all the little spaces that occurred between the remarkable days in the calendar with proverbial sentences, chiefly such as inculcat'd industry and frugality, as the means of procuring wealth, and thereby securing virtue; it being more difficult for a man in want, to act always honestly, as, to use here one of those proverbs, 'It is hard for an empty sack to stand upright.' "

The first advertisement for *Poor Richard* was published in the *Pennsylvania Gazette* on December 19, 1732 "... Just published for 1733, an Almanack, containing the Luminations, Eclipses, Planets' Motions and Aspects, Sun and Moon's Rising and Setting, Weather, High Water, Etc.; besides many pleasant and witty Verses, Jests, and sayings ... By Richard Saunders, Philomat. Printed and sold by B. FRANKLIN."

Preferring to continue"out of sight"Ben adopted Richard Saunders as his pseudonym. Whatever wit, wisdom and humor reflected to the almanac came from the amply knowledgeable pen of *Poor Richard* himself.

In all honesty, though, we can't give Ben credit for inventing either Richard Saunders or *Poor Richard*.

Richard Saunders was, in fact, a seventeenth century English astronomer, compiler of the *Apollo Anglicanus*. While *Poor Richard* derived from "Poor Robin," an almanac published by James Franklin [2] at his new shop in Newport, Rhode Island. Nor can he claim credit as the originator of hundreds upon hundreds of witticisms ascribed to him, through *Poor Richard*, during the almanac's twenty-five years in circulation.

But we must, nevertheless, give Ben his due. His innovative approach to his almanac added appeal to the somewhat stodgy almanacs of the day. Readers looked forward to its yearly issue. And, by 1748, *Poor Richard* had become an institution. That year ten thousand copies were sold, with the same number sold yearly until it ceased publication in 1758. *Poor Richard's Almanac* was the most popular reading material in the colonies. Second only to the *Holy Bible*.

Chapter 2

Ben, in creating the character of *Poor Richard* had assumed its' identity. As with Silence Dogood [1] he wanted to speak out, but again feared the public would not listen to him in his own person. Silence Dogood was silenced forever. *Poor Rickard* was not.

As *Poor Richard*, he pretended at astrology, yet made fun of superstition. He pretended to be old and wise, packing his almanac with sagacity of the ages. He spoke of prudence, industry and frugality. He wrote as a moralist admonishing mankind for its lack of order, while upholding that for mankind to succeed depended upon men looking out for themselves; that man should work to be happy, and save to be secure. He wrote that industry and frugality were the natural roads to freedom.

Though *Poor Richard* took his wit and wisdom from such notables as John Dryden, Alexander Pope, Thomas Fuller, Jonathan Swift, Francis Bacon, Francois dé La Rochefoucauld, Francois Rebelais and many others, Ben did not copy their compositions. Instead, he reworded them to suit his purpose and that of his readers. "Writing,"he contended,"should be'smooth, clear, and short.' "

In 1732, Thomas Fuller wrote "It is better to have a hen to-morrow, than an egg to-day." Ben revamped it in 1734 to read "A hen to-day is better than an egg to-morrow."

In 1742, he laughingly reworked an old verse to poke fun at himself:

> *"Ben beats his pate and fancies wit will come.*
> *But he may knock, there's nobody at home."*

Some sage advice which made *Poor Richard* famous in his day and Ben Franklin remembered today, were published between 1733 and 1758:

Forewarn'd, forearm'd.
Diligence is the mother of good-luck.
Keep thy shop, and thy shop will keep thee.
Necessity never made a good bargain.
Eat to please thyself, but dress to please others.
He that falls in love with himself, will have no rivals.
Money and good manners make the gentleman.
When the well's dry, we know the worth of water.
Lost time is never found again.
Having been poor is no shame,being asham'd of it is.
A pair of good ears will drain a hundred tongues.
Love thy neighbor; yet don't pull down your hedge.
The way to be safe, is not to be secure.

Benjamin Franklin, however, was not the only historical figure to transcend maxims.

In 1750, *Poor Richard* wrote "You may be too cunning for one, but not for all." Nearly 113 years later, Abraham Lincoln gave us his own revision:
"You may fool all of the people some of the time;
you can even fool some of the people all of the time;
but you can't fool all of the people all of the time."

"A generous heart, kind speech, and life of service and compassion are the things that renew humanity."
Siddhārtha Gautama
Buddha
Founder of Buddhism
(563 B.C.E. – 483 B.C.E.)

Chapter 3

*P*oor Richard had a tremendous impact on the lives of aspiring Americans in the eighteenth century. It was a century of hope — and of opportunity for the economically oppressed. Its people sought in *Poor Richard*'s examples and proverbs the formula for success. They embraced, especially, those sayings which emphasized diligence, frugality and thrift.

Unfortunately, as the eighteenth turned into the 19th and 20th centuries, get-rich-quick schemes and scams began to surface throughout the world. Boys, whose fathers and grandfathers held with Franklin's views, grew believing the"fast buck"their only means to affluence. This outlook passed to their descendants. As a result, many lost. Their attempts to "beat the system" were met with dismal failure.

Franklin, in the guise of *Poor Richard*, was speaking from his own experiences and difficulties up to 1730, when he had been a failure himself.   The original words may have come from a Fuller or Bacon, but the thoughts were from his own lot.

Not until 1730 did he realize his need to follow the plan written four years earlier [1]. With a new business, a new wife and son, came a new sense of responsibility.

When at length he mastered the plan, he resolved to deliver its impressions to his readers "...that they might achieve some measure of success, and rise to prominence in the world."

"He that can have patience," he had written in 1726, "can have what he will."

He was, by now, following his own counsel.

As the years passed and *Poor Richard* prospered, so also did his readers. Not only were they shown how to earn money,they were given information on making wine from wild grapes and what timber to use for better fencing. They were advised to weather changes for an abundant crop season, and introduced to a new-style calendar [2].

When *Poor Richard's Almanac* first came out, it was the eighth almanac in Philadelphia. By 1758, it was the best selling of all the almanacs throughout the world.

Total sales: Over a quarter of a million copies.

Even France had taken *Poor Richard* to heart, renaming him "*Bon Hommé Richard*."

The French merchant class, having grown weary of aristocracy and its heavy-handedness toward individual pursuits, read every issue of the translated almanac from cover to cover.

Meetings were held.
Both merchants and their citizen patrons gathered to hear passages read aloud.
Everywhere, the cry went out:

"Free enterprise is the way to wealth.
Down with the aristocratic weight of Taxes!"

The people of France had a new hero. A hero destined to eventually lead them, if in spirit only, to their own revolution...

And so. As we look back on a chaotic past, we look forward to a unified future. A future which will take us within reach of a final quest of mankind. A quest so long to arrive, yet so long needed if we are expected to survive as a species.

Our religious and secular factions are attempting to bond into an ethical union. Whether theocentric or humanistic is irrelevant in wording. In action, we are viewing the formation of what may become a lasting covenant with God in our daily lives and enterprises.

Moving into its third thousand years, maybe we are learning Christianity in its true sense. There is nothing unethical with earthly power if that power is practiced fairly, and does not render hurt and humiliation to those under its influence. Too, there is nothing unethical in commercial profits if acquired honestly and equitably. God has never questioned power or money. Only to its obtainment and ultimate distribution.

Decidedly, we must perceive, accept and seize an elemental reality to life's creed...

In a virtual world, we may stroll — Christian, Jewish, Buddhist, Moslem, believers and non-believers, religious leaders and secular — hand-in-hand along a flowery path toward a singular heavenly light.

But in the real world, merely standing together should be sufficient to satisfy the final quest for **God's Truth**!

Miscellaneous

"It is one of the most beautiful compensations of life that no man [or woman] can sincerely try to help another without helping himself."
Ralph Waldo Emerson
American essayist, philosopher, poet
(1803 – 1882)

Chapter Notes

A Quest For Absolute Power

Chapter 1:

1. Administrative body of the Roman Catholic Church.

Chapter 3:

1. Referring to Rome (Roman Curia).
2. St. John Chrysostom (ca 347 – 404) Greek Orthodox church father. Archbishop of Constantinople.
3. Roman Catholic Church.
4. Pope Clement VII [1523 – 1534], cousin to Pope Leo X [1513 – 1521].

Chapter 4:

1. Second Vatican Council. Opened by Pope John XXIII, the Second Ecumenical Council of the Vatican invited all Christian churches to observe it "…throw open the windows of the Church so that we can see out and the people can see in."
2. Mehmet Ali Ağca was held in Rome's Rebibbia Prison. After serving nineteen months of his sentence, he was pardoned at the behest of Pope John Paul II. Then extradited to Turkey on a separate charge of robbery and murder.
3. A planned series of terrorist attacks, basically consisting of three separate plots: (1) Pope John Paul II's assassination on January 15th. (2) The bombing of eleven airlines, scheduled for January 21st and 22nd. (3) Flying a Cessna filled with explosives into C.I.A Headquarters, Langley, VA.
4. Pastoral Staff, usually shaped as a shepherd's crook, is an ecclesiastical ornament conferred on bishops when consecrated and abbots at their investiture. Presently, the pope does not use the crosier. However, for Pope John Paul II its use was necessary and forgiven.

The Final Quest

Chapter 1:

1. Originally spelled *Poor Richard's Almanack*.
2. Ben Franklin's older brother.

Chapter 2:

1. A fictional character created by Ben Franklin when a teenager.

Chapter 3:

1. A plan for self-improvement augmented to his journal [diary] in 1726.
2. The Gregorian calendar. In use today.

"When you were born, you cried and the world rejoiced. Live your life so that when you die, the world cries and you rejoice."

Cherokee Proverb

Religious Trivia

Did you know:

Gabriel, Michael and Lucifer are the only angels mentioned by name in the Bible.

The Aramaic language of the ancient Bible did not have a translation for the phrase "many things." Usage for this term came down to us as "forty." Therefore, the "forty days" mentioned on several occasions in both the Old and New Testament refers to "many days."

Approximately fifty men authored the Bible over a sixteen hundred-year period, dating from 1500 B.C.E. to a little over one hundred years after Christ.

Approximately forty different authors wrote the sixty-six books of King James' Bible.

The Bible devotes five hundred verses on prayer, less than five hundred on faith, and over two thousand on money and possessions.

Although not named in the New Testament, traditional history cites the two thieves crucified with Jesus as Dismas and Gestes.

The patron saint of dentistry is St. Apollonia who, according to legend, suffered martyrdom by violently having her teeth pulled out by a mob of anti-Christians in 249 C.E.

Gnosticism, meaning a possession of mystical knowledge, was a type of Christian faith deemed heresy by early Roman Church authorities.

Pope Leo I ["The Great" — 440 – 461] was so feared by Attila the Hun, the Huns' king reconsidered plans to invade Rome in 452 C.E.

Dionysius Exiguus (ca 470 – ca 544), a 6th century monk, created the B.C./A.D. dating system in 525. Today, we use B.C.E. [Before the Common Era] and C.E. [Common Era] as a scholastic dating system.

A woman named Joan [various names are given her, depending on the legend] reigned as Pope John VIII from 853 to 855, her gender revealed only by giving birth to a stillborn child during a Papal procession on the road from St. Peter's Basilica to the Patriarchium [now St. John's Lateran] in full view of the Roman public.

Upon discovering the pope's true gender an incensed mob tied the woman's feet together, dragged her behind a horse, and stoned her until she died.

Another story has "Pope Joan" deposed after the birth and banished to a distant convent for a life of penance, where she would watch her son grow to take the position of Bishop of Ostia, thirty miles southwest of Rome.

When nearing death, she requested her body be interred on the road where her child had been delivered.

Her son, however, refused this and removed her remains to the Cathedral in Ostia for burial with honor. "God," it was accounted by a 14th century historian, "has worked many miracles [in this place] to the present day."

There has been disputable evidence both for and against the existence of Joan as the original Pope John VIII.

Still, we just do not have enough contemporary confirmation for an effective argument either way.

Perhaps the 19th century French author/historian, Auguste Vallet dé Viriville (1815 – 1868), said it best:

"Whenever you see a legend, you can be sure, if you go to the bottom of things, that you will find history."

"Pope Joan" (as Pope John VIII)
leading a Papal procession.
Courtesy:
U.S. News & World Report
1050 Thomas Jefferson Street NW
Washington, D.C. 20007

The real Pope John VIII [872 – 882], extremely effeminate but cruel, was the first pontiff assassinated. He was poisoned, then beaten to death when the deadly liquid took too long for effect.

Pope Stephen VI [896 – 897] had the decomposing body of Pope Formosus [891 – 896] exhumed and put on trial for alleged offenses committed during his reign. This led to his own arrest, imprisonment, and execution via strangulation.

Pope Urban II [1088 – 1099] established the **Roman Curia** to administer the Papal court.

Pope Innocent III's [1198 – 1216] papacy led to legalization of the Inquisition of 1223, which firmly established the heretical investigations and trials by Pope Gregory IX [1227 – 1241] in 1231, which in turn led to the burnings of an unjustly condemned John Huss (1371 – 1415) and the equally innocent Joan of Arc (ca 1412 – 1431) in the 15th century.

The first Middle English translations of the Bible were initiated by John Wycliffe (ca 1320 – 1384) in 1382 and completed by his assistant, John Purvey (1353 – 1428) from 1388 to 1395.

These translations principally induced the pre-Reformation movement, which rejected injurious activities by the Roman Catholic Church.

John Huss [also spelled Jan Hus],who would suffer a martyred death in 1415, clung to Wycliffe's beliefs in calling for Protestant reform — predating Martin Luther.

During his trial for actions against the Roman Church, in

June of 1415, Huss conceded veneration of Wycliffe and volunteered this statement: "I can only wish my soul can sometime attain unto that place where Wycliff's is."

This angered the judging Council of Constance. John Wycliffe was a heretic who escaped punishment by dying too early and Purvey, his faint-hearted assistant, was still in hiding.

Exasperated, they handed Huss a list of confessions but he refused to recant what he knew was not true and "against my conscience." Instead, he asked that they strike from the list those doctrines which he had never taught and considered erroneous.

Staring down on the accused, the assemblage shook its collective head.

He would recant everything put before him, they ordered, or undergo the consequences.

Huss still refused to disavow his beliefs.

On July 6, 1415, he was burned alive with degradation; a tall, pointed, hat placed on his head, as he was disrobed and the kindling lit.

As the flames engulfed his body, he praised John Wycliffe and rang out the words: "In 100 years, God will raise up a man whose calls for reform cannot be suppressed."

One hundred and two years later, Martin Luther began his maneuvers to reform the Roman Catholic Church in Wittenberg, Germany.

On May 4, 1415, the Council of Constance had decreed John Wycliffe "a heretic without repentance" and drew up an order, which stood on the shelf for twelve years...

Finally responding to the order in 1428, Pope Martin V [1417 – 1431] commanded Wycliffe's remains exhumed and burned to ashes, then cast into the river Swift — in hopes his life of trouble to the Church would be forgotten.

John Wycliffe's bones were burned and cast out.
From: *Actes and Monuments*
[Also known as: *Foxe's Book of Martyrs*]
Printed and published by John Day, 1563.

"Already a third and more of England is in the hands of the Pope. There cannot be two temporal sovereigns in one country; either Edward is king or Urban is king. We make our choice. We accept Edward of England and refute Urban of Rome."

John Wycliffe
"Morning Star of the Reformation"

In 1455, Pope Callixtus III [1455 – 1459] authorized Joan of Arc's "Nullification Trial" at the request of the new Grand Inquisitor Jean Bréhal and Joan's mother, Isabelle Romée.

Joan was found innocent of all charges on July 7, 1456.

"Joan," Bréhal had summarized during the retrial, "was a martyr, and I charge the late Pierre Cauchon with heresy for convicting an innocent woman in pursuit of a secular vendetta."

Joan was beatified by Pope Pius X [1903 – 1914] on April 18, 1909 and canonized by Pope Benedict XV [1914 – 1922] on May 16, 1920.

"Jehanne"
Signature of Joan of Arc
From a letter dictated to:
Henry VI, king of England.

"One life is all we have and we live it as we believe in living it. But to sacrifice what we are and live without belief, that is a fate more terrible than dying."
Joan of Arc
[Jeanne d'Arc]

Religious Reading

You can borrow the following excellent religious books [some rare, some on DVD] from larger public libraries. Or purchase from a new and used book dealer.

Buddhism:

- *Modern Buddhism*/ Alan James

- *The Buddhist Directory*/ Richard Landau (ed.)

- *Living Zen*/ Robert Linssen

- *The Way of Zen*/ Alan W. Watts

➢ *Buddha's Philosophy of Man*/ Trevor Ling (ed.)

➢ *Buddhism: An Introduction and Guide*/ Christmas Humphreys

➢ *Compassion and the Individuals*/ Bstan-Dzin-Rgya-Mtsho

➢ *Buddhism: The Path to Nirvana [Religion Traditions of the world]*/ Robert Lester

➢ *Buddha and the Gospel of Buddhism*/ Ananda K. Coomaraswamy

➢ *Basic Buddhist Concepts*/ Kogen Mizumo

➢ *Manual of Zen Buddhism*/ D.T. Suzuki

➢ *Answers: Discussions With Western Buddhists*/ The Dalai Lama

Catholicism:

➢ *The Role of the Christian Family in the Modern World*/ Pope John Paul II

➢ *The Gospel Without Compromise*/ Catherine De Hueck Doherty

➢ *It Is I Who Have Chosen You*/ Judie Brown

- ➤ *Act of Contrition: Personal Responsibility and sin/* Jeffrey Sobosan

- ➤ *Fashion Me A People: Man, Woman and the Church/* Eugene C. Kennedy

- ➤ *Mosquitoes in Paradise: A New Look at Genesis, Jesus, and the Meaning of Life/* John R. Aurelio

- ➤ *Personhood: The Art of Being Fully Human/* Leo F. Buscaglia

- ➤ *Receiving the Promise: The Spirit's Work of Conver-Sion/* Thomas G. Weinandy

- ➤ *A Summary of the Seven Sacraments/* Daughters of St. Paul

- ➤ *Dialogue: Reflections on God and Man/* Pope Paul VI

- ➤ *On Social Concern: Encyclical Letter of John Paul II/* Pope John Paul II

General Christianity:

- ➤ *More Than Coping/* Elizabeth Skoglund

- ➤ *Honest to God? Becoming an Authentic Christian/* Bill Hybels

- ➢ *The Church and Family*/ J.D. Middlebrook & Larry Summers

- ➢ *Enthusiasm Makes the Difference*/ Norman Vincent Peale

- ➢ *Living More With Less: Study Action Guide*/ Delores Friesen

- ➢ *The God Chasers — My Soul Follows Hard After Thee*/ Tommy Tenney

- ➢ *Ongoing Journey: Women and the Bible*/ Sharon Neufer Emswiler

- ➢ *The Positive Power of Jesus Christ*/ Norman Vincent Peale

- ➢ *The Art of Christian Meditation: A Guide to Increase Your Personal Awareness of God*/ David A. Ray

- ➢ *Living Beyond Our Fears: Discovering Life When You're Scared to Death*/ Bruce Larson

Hinduism:

- ➢ *The Quest for Enlightenment*/ A. C. Bhaktivedanta Swami Prbhupada

- ➢ *Hinduism [Great Religions of Modern Man Series]*/ Louis Renou

- *A Source Book of Modern Hinduism*/ Glyn Richards

- *Hinduism, The World's Oldest Faith*/ K.M. Sen

- *Gandhi Through Western Eyes*/ Horace Alexander

- *Hinduism*/ R.C. Zachner

- *Path to Oriental Wisdom: Introductory Studies in Eastern Philosophy*/ George Parulski

- *Mind: It's Mysteries and Control*/ Swami Sivananda

- *Hinduism and Buddhism*/ Ananda K. Coomaraswamy

- *Outline of Hinduism*/ F. Howard Smith

Islam:

- *The Conception of God in Islam*/ Kadar

- *Islam*/ Alfred Guillaume

- *Understanding Islam*/ Thomas W. Lippman

- *Mohammedism*/ H.A.R. Gibb

- *Islam [Great Religions of Modern Man Series]*/ John Alden Williams (ed.)

➤ *Islam In Modern History/* Wilfred Cartwell Smith

➤ *Mediators Between Human and Devine: From Moses to Mohammed/* John Macquarrie

➤ *Islam in the World/* Malise Ruthven

➤ *Islam: Beliefs and Obsessions/* Caesar F. Farah

➤ *Mohammed, the Man and His Faith/* Andr, Tor, Bp.

➤ *The Koran/* N.J. Dawood (translator)

Judaism:

➤ *Judaism [Great Religions of Modern Man Series]/* Arthur Hertzberg (ed.)

➤ *Spiritual Trails to Happiness/* Solomon Foster

➤ *Passover: A Popular History of Jewish Civilization/* Mordell Klein

➤ *Celebrating Life: Jewish Rites of Passage/* Malka Drucker

➤ *Liberal Judaism at Home: The Practices of Modern Judaism/* Morrison David Bial

➤ *The Jewish Woman: New Perspectives/* Elizabeth Koltum

- *Anne Frank: The Diary of a Young Girl*/ Anne Frank

- *The Story of Passover*/ Bobbie Katz

- *To Life!: A Celebration of Jewish Being and Thinking*/ Harold Kushner

- *Footsteps to Freedom*/ Levi O. Keidel

- *Great Jewish Short Stories*/ Saul Bellow (ed.)

- *Share the New Life with a Jew*/ Moishe Rosen

Protestantism:

- *A Plea for Faith*/ Stuart A. Garver

- *How to Be a Christian Without Being Religious*/ Regal Publications

- *The Churches' Handbook for Spiritual Healing*/ Walter Dwyer

- *Following God's Way: Our Perfect Example*/ Phyllis Bennett

- *The Reformation...then and Now*/ Charles S. Anderson

- *Heroes of the Faith*/ Dr. C.S. Knapp

- ➤ *Understanding the Judgment Seat of Christ: The Believer's Accountability*/ Randy Schoepflin

- ➤ *How... A Series of Vital and Practical Studies Relating to the Christian Life*/ Southern Bible Books

- ➤ *Personal Factors in Character Building*/ John Milburn Price

- ➤ *A Woman's Path to Godliness*/ Martha Reapsome

Religious Education:

- ➤ *Women in the Pulpit: Is God an Equal Opportunity Employer?*/ Proctor Pam & Proctor William

- ➤ *Preparing for Liturgy: A Theology and Spirituality*/ Austin Fleming

- ➤ *Helping Youth in Conflict*/ Francis I. Frelick

- ➤ *If Ministries Fall, Can They Be Restored?*/ Tim LaHay

- ➤ *Boundaries of the Soul: The Practice of Jung's Psychology*/ June Singer

- ➤ *God's Answer to Anxiety*/ B.W. Woods

- ➤ *Living Through Personal Crises*/ Ann Kaiser Sterns

Religious Reading

- ➤ *A Plain Man Faces Trouble* / Weldon O. Wilson

- ➤ *Metaphysics*/ E. Ray Clendermen & Richard A. Taylor

- ➤ *Freedom to Fail*/ Don G. Gilmore

- ➤ *What Everyone Should know about Transcendental Meditation*/ Gordon Russell Lewis

"Action may not always bring happiness, but there is no happiness without action."
Benjamin Disraeli
British statesman
(1804 – 1881)

Bibliography

No writing effort can ever begin without extensive research. Whether we agree with past renderings is irrelevant, since it is left for the present author to garner whatever material found available and return a determination of reliability.

Although this is admittedly not a large theological treatise, the below represents but a small portion of the books and papers studied during its preparation.

All were thoroughly examined and cross-referenced for as much an accurate analysis as is possible.

Atkinson, James. *Martin Luther and the Birth of Protestantism*. Westminster John Knox Press, London, 1982.

Ayer, William Ward. *God's Answer to Man's Doubts*. Zondervan Publishing House, Grand Rapids, MI, 1942.

Blair, Joseph L. *Cornerstones of Religious Freedom*. The Beacon Press, Boston, MA, 1949.

Brown, George Kenneth. *Italy and the Restoration to 1550*. Russell & Russell Publishing, Oxford, 1971.

Chadwick, H. *The Early Christian Church*. London, 1970.

Chamberlin, Eric Russell. *The Bad Popes*. Dial Press, Inc., New York, 1969.

Conzelmann, Hans & Steely, John E. *History of Primitive Christianity*. Abington Press, 1973.

Coulton, C.G. *The Inquisition*. London, 1974.

Dawson, Christopher. *The Dividing of Christendom*.

De Rosa, Peter. *Vicars of Christ: The Darkside of the Papacy*. Poolbeg Press, Dublin, Ireland, 2000.

Eliade, M. *The Encyclopedia of Religion*. McMillian Publishing Co., Inc., New York, 1967.

Eric, John. *The Popes*. Hawthorn Crook, 1964.

Bibliography

Foxe, John. *Actes and Monuments of These Latter and Perilous Days, touching Matters of the Church* [also known as *Foxe's Book of Martyrs*]. Printed and published by John Daly, 1563.

Goodspeed, Edgar J. *How Come the Bible?* Abbington - Cokesbury Press, New York, 1944.

Hamilton, Bernard. *The Mediaeval Inquisition*. Holmes & Meier Publishers, Inc., London, 1982.

Henter, Jan Willem Van & Avemarie, Frederick. *Martyrdom and Noble Death*. Routledge, 2002.

Jacobs, Charles M. *The Story of the Church*. The Muhlenburg Press, Philadelphia, PA, 1949.

Johnson, Paul. *Pope John Paul II and the Catholic Restoration*. St. Martin's Press, London, 1982.

Kamen, H. *The Spanish Inquisition*. New American Library, New York, 1965.

Kennedy, George Alexander. *Classical Rhetoric and its Christian and Secular Tradition from Ancient to Modern Times*.

University of North Carolina Press, 1980.

Knutson, G. *The Cross and the Crown*. Our Savior's Lutheran Church, Austin, MI, 1990.

Latourette, Kenneth S. *A History of Christianity*. Harper's Press, 1975.

Pagels, Elaine. *The Gnostic Gospels*. Vintage Books, New York, 1989.

Rand, Edward Kennard. *Founders of the Middle Ages*. Dover Publications, New York, 1957.

Smoley, Richard. *Inner Christianity: A Guide to the Esoteric Tradition*. Shambhala, Boston, 2002.

Vailancourt, Jean-Guy. *Papal Power*. University of California Press, 1980.

Vos, Howard F. *Highlights of Church History*. Moody Press, Chicago, IL, 1960.

Williams, George H. *The Mind of John Paul II*. Seabury Press, New York, 1981.

Index

An italicized *n* following a page number is a chapter note.

"The time has come to educate people to cease all quarrels in the name of religion, culture, countries, different political or economical systems. Fighting is useless. Suicide."

14th Dalai Lama

Tenzin Gyatso

(b. 1935 –)

As quoted on September 8, 2006 in:

The Globe and Mail

444 Front Street, West

Toronto, ON M5V 2S9

About the Author

Dr. Bouffard holds an LL.B. from LaSalle University, a Masters and Psy.D. from Neotarian College of Psychology. And has applied thirty years to psychological counseling.

In 1999, he earned a Ph.D. (a candidacy shelved for over twenty years due to time restraints) in Theocentric Business and Ethics from American College of Metaphysical Theology, leading to ministerial credentials.

Currently, he is devoting much of his time to writing historical books and informational manuals, and managing a supportive Internet presence called *Doc Jim's Help Page!*